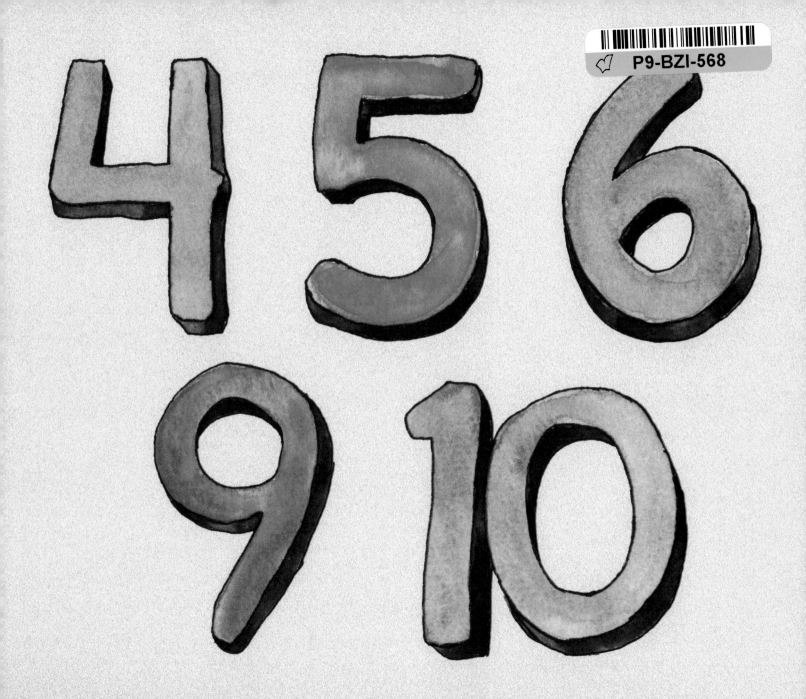

No part of this publication may be reproduced in whole or in part,
or stored in a retrieval system, or transmitted in any form or by any means,
electronic, mechanical, photocopying, recording, or otherwise,
without written permission of the publisher.
For information regarding permission, write to: Scholastic Inc.,
Attention: Permissions Department, 557 Broadway, New York, NY 10012.

Published by Scholastic Inc.,
90 Old Sherman Turnpike, Danbury, Connecticut 06816.

SCHOLASTIC and associated logos are trademarks
and/or registered trademarks of Scholastic Inc.

ISBN 0-7172-8614-2

Printed in the U.S.A.

First Scholastic Printing, August 2005

My seven Book

by Jane Belk Moncure
illustrated by Ben Mahan

SCHOLASTIC INC.

New York   Toronto   London   Auckland   Sydney
Mexico City   New Delhi   Hong Kong   Buenos Aires

This is Little  .

Little  lives in the house of seven.

It has seven rooms. Count them.

Every day Little  goes for a walk.

One day he walks in the park.

He sees one big duck . . .

and six little
ducks
in a pond.

How many ducks all together?

Some ducks say, *Quack, quack, quack.*

Some ducks dive under the water.
They are looking for snails.

Can you count how many heads
and how many tails?

Next Little  sees frogs on a log.

He counts four . . .

and three more.

How many frogs all together?

Little 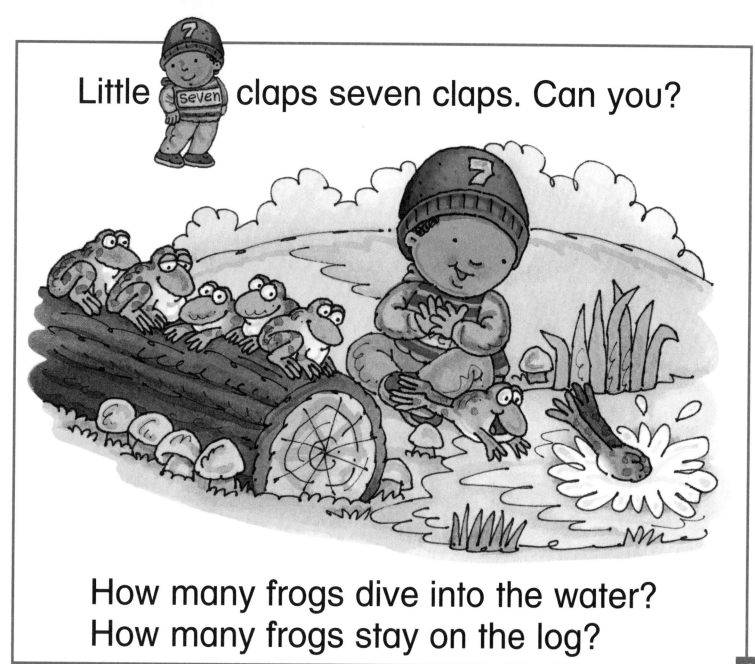 seven claps seven claps. Can you?

How many frogs dive into the water?
How many frogs stay on the log?

Little Seven walks past the pond.
He comes . . .

to a big stump.

He sees a mama turtle and lots
of little turtles. Count them.

Little  finds a net.

He catches the little turtles.

How many did he catch? How many turtles are left?

The little turtles are sad. So Little  seven lets them go home to their Mama.

Now count the happy turtles.

Next Little  sees a big mound of sticks. "I will sit and rest," he says.

But a beaver peeks its head out.
"You are sitting on my house," it says.

Little seven jumps away. Out come

two big
beavers . . .

and five little beavers. How many beavers are in the whole family?

"Watch us play," they say.

Little  says, "I will play, too."

He jumps seven times. Can you?
Guess what he finds.

He finds a big sandbox with a toy train in it.

How many cars is the engine pulling?

Little  Seven builds a track for the train.

Then he makes a tunnel.

"I will pull the seven cars through the tunnel," he says.

Little  pulls. Does the whole train come through the tunnel?

"It is getting late. I must go home," says Little .

On his way home, Little  seven sees some pennies.

How many coins does he find all together?

Little  seven hops to a shop.

He looks in the window.
He sees lots of lollipops.

A sign says: **Lollipops 1 penny each** .

"Whee!" says Little .
"I can buy lots of

lollipops. I have seven pennies."
How many lollipops can he buy?

26

He buys three cherry lollipops
and four grape lollipops.
Count them.

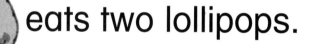

Little seven eats two lollipops.

How many does he leave for you?

Little  finds seven of everything.

seven
ducks

seven
beavers

seven
turtles

seven
train
cars

seven
lollipops

Now you find seven things.

Little 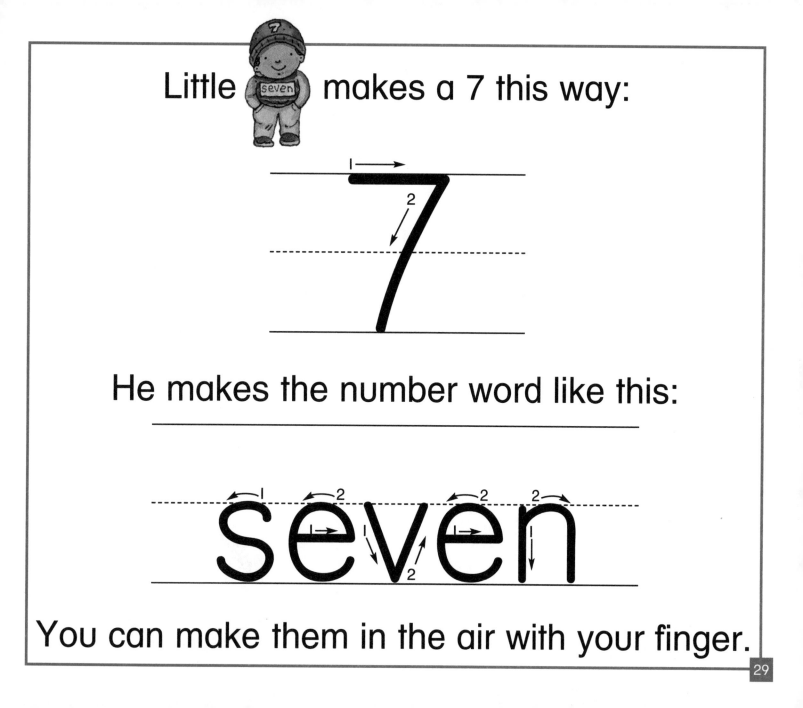 makes a 7 this way:

7

He makes the number word like this:

seven

You can make them in the air with your finger.